Penguin Readers

A SOLSTICE AT STONEHENGE

ANNA TREWIN

LEVEL

ILLUSTRATED BY KATIE WOOD
SERIES EDITOR: SORREL PITTS

PENGUIN BOOKS

UK | USA | Canada | Ireland | Australia
India | New Zealand | South Africa

Penguin Books is part of the Penguin Random House group of companies
whose addresses can be found at global.penguinrandomhouse.com.
www.penguin.co.uk www.puffin.co.uk www.ladybird.co.uk

First published 2026
001

Text written by Anna Trewin
Text copyright © Penguin Books Ltd, 2026
Illustrated by Katie Wood
Illustrations copyright © Penguin Books Ltd, 2026
Cover illustrated by Shahid Mahmood and Katie Wood

Penguin Random House values and supports copyright. Copyright fuels creativity, encourages diverse voices, promotes freedom of expression and supports a vibrant culture. Thank you for purchasing an authorized edition of this book and for respecting intellectual property laws by not reproducing, scanning or distributing any part of it by any means without permission. You are supporting authors and enabling Penguin Random House to continue to publish books for everyone. No part of this book may be used or reproduced in any manner for the purpose of training artificial intelligence technologies or systems. In accordance with Article 4(3) of the DSM Directive 2019/790, Penguin Random House expressly reserves this work from the text and data mining exception.

Printed and bound in Great Britain by Clays Ltd, Elcograf S.p.A.

The authorized representative in the EEA is Penguin Random House Ireland, Morrison Chambers,
32 Nassau Street, Dublin D02 YH68

A CIP catalogue record for this book is available from the British Library

ISBN: 978–0–241–75374–3

All correspondence to:
Penguin Books
Penguin Random House Children's
One Embassy Gardens, 8 Viaduct Gardens,
London SW11 7BW

Penguin Random House is committed to a
sustainable future for our business, our
readers and our planet. This book is made
from Forest Stewardship Council® certified

Contents

People in the story	4
New words	5
Places in the story	6
Note about the story	8
Before-reading questions	8
Chapter One – City girl	9
Chapter Two – A journey to the stones	14
Chapter Three – The path around the stones	20
Chapter Four – The exhibition	31
Chapter Five – Back home	39
Chapter Six – The solstice	46
Chapter Seven – Everything is possible	54
During-reading questions	56
After-reading questions	57
Exercises	57
Project work	61
Glossary	62

People in the story

Isabel Ryan

Jasmine

Shaheed

Simon

Miss Novak

Mr and Mrs Ryan

New words

circle

field

hill

sunrise

tourist

visitor centre

Places in the story

Stonehenge

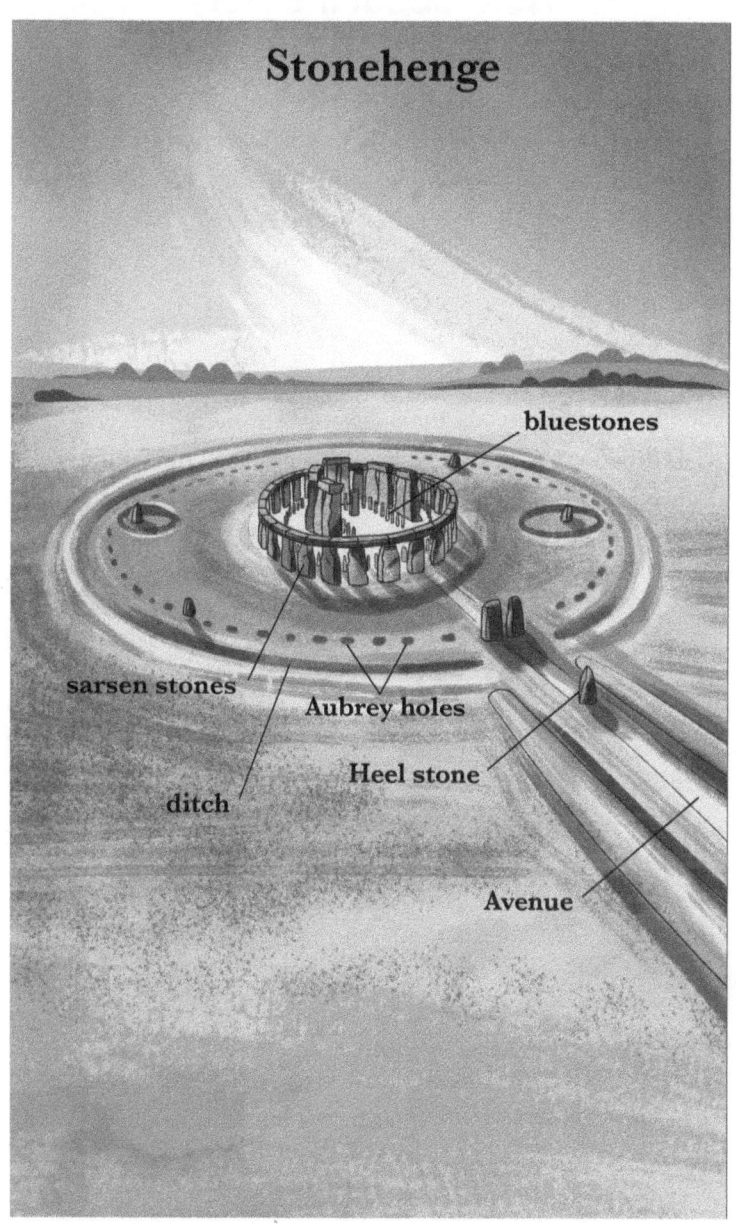

Note about the story

Stonehenge is a famous **stone*** circle in Wiltshire, in the south of England. It is 5,000 years old. Its builders **aligned** the stones with the sunrises of the winter solstice (the shortest day and longest night of the year) and summer solstice (the longest day and shortest night). Every year, thousands of people visit Stonehenge, and many come for the solstices.

Stonehenge has a big visitor centre and **exhibition** hall. People must get their tickets from the visitor centre, and then a bus takes them to the stones. The stones are about two miles from the centre. People usually visit the exhibition after the stones.

Before-reading questions

1 Look at the cover of the book. What do you know about Stonehenge?
2 Read the "Note about the story" on this page. What happens to the days and nights on the winter and summer solstices?

*Definitions of words in **bold** can be found in the glossary on pages 62–63.

CHAPTER ONE
City girl

"Look, everyone – look!" says Miss Novak. She points out of the bus window. "It's Stonehenge! We're nearly here!"

Isabel looks up from her phone and out of the window. There are only fields in the morning sun.

"You're looking out of the wrong side of the bus, city girl," says a boy called Simon. Isabel does not like Simon very much. He is never very nice to her. Simon is sitting with his friend Shaheed in the **seat** behind. Isabel turns and looks through their window, but there are only more fields.

"Too late. We went by Stonehenge," says Jasmine. She is sitting next to Isabel. Jasmine is nice, but Isabel does not know her very well. She does not know any of the students well because she is new to St Anne's School. She came to Wiltshire from Birmingham with her parents in February, and she **misses** the city. The **countryside** is **boring**.

Her parents' village is very quiet and pretty – but there is nothing to do there.

Isabel looks back at her phone. There is lots of **chat** and photos from her friends in Birmingham, but no one asks about her **journey** to Stonehenge. "Are they forgetting me?" she **worries**.

"I'm very **excited**," says Jasmine. "Stonehenge looks wonderful in the photos. We're going to have a great day."

"No, we're not. We're going to have a boring day in the countryside," Isabel thinks. "I want to be with my friends in Birmingham. I don't want to be in a field of stupid **stones**."

Coming to Stonehenge was Miss Novak's idea. Miss Novak teaches **history** at St Anne's School.

"You must go," said Isabel's mother. "Stonehenge is a wonderful place. And the journey there is **really** beautiful."

"Mum was wrong. This journey is really boring," Isabel thinks now. "It's just road after road and field after field."

The bus turns on to a smaller road. "We're nearly there," says Jasmine.

"I hate the countryside!" says Isabel.

Jasmine laughs. "You only know cities," she says. "This is Wiltshire. The countryside here is beautiful and **ancient**. And Stonehenge is a very famous place. You'll understand soon."

"No, I won't," thinks Isabel.

But Isabel is not only unhappy because of Stonehenge and the countryside. "I miss my friends in Birmingham," she thinks. "But my **grades** were bad, and I was **bored** in class. Mum and Dad were **worried** about me, and they came to Wiltshire. OK, Mum's also got a better job here. But they really came because of me."

Isabel looks out of the window again, and then at Jasmine. "Jasmine gets good grades, but my grades at St Anne's are as bad as before. School is boring. It was boring in Birmingham, and it's boring in Wiltshire too."

The students get off the bus in front of the visitor centre and wait in a group. There are about ten of them, and they are all in Miss Novak's class. Simon and Shaheed are as bored as Isabel. They start playing a game on Shaheed's phone.

Jasmine stays next to Isabel. "Do you like Miss Novak?" she asks.

"She's OK," answers Isabel.

"She finished **university** last year. She's a very new teacher," says Jasmine. "She's really nice. We'll learn lots of things today."

"Jasmine is a **nerd**," Isabel thinks.

CHAPTER TWO
A journey to the stones

A bus comes and stops next to the visitor centre. It has the word "STONEHENGE" above the driver's seat. The students and Miss Novak get on the bus. Lots of other people get on it too. There are other children and teachers, and lots of tourists with cameras. There are people here from Japan, Australia, Germany, the United States of America and many other countries.

"How many miles is it to the stones, Miss?" Jasmine asks.

"It's under two miles," says Miss Novak.

The bus begins to move slowly on the road, and Isabel is not bored now. It is a warm May day, and the countryside **around** her looks very ancient and beautiful. She sees some small hills in the middle of a big field.

"What are those strange hills, Miss?" she asks.

"Those are the Cursus Barrows," answers Miss Novak. "The Neolithic people built the barrows and **buried** their dead people in them. Later, the Bronze Age people built barrows too. There are many barrows around Stonehenge."

The bus takes Miss Novak and her class up the long, straight road. They want to see the stones, but there are too many trees. Everyone on the bus is excited. They are all talking very fast.

Suddenly, the bus comes through the trees, and they see a **huge** circle of tall grey stones on the **horizon.**

Everyone on the bus stops talking, their mouths open. Some of the stones are standing, and they have stones on top of them. There are more stones inside the circle. Some of them are large and some are smaller. Many stones lie on the ground.

"What a beautiful, ancient place," Isabel says.

"Better than Birmingham, city girl," says Simon.

Isabel is angry, but she does not answer Simon.

Miss Novak looks at Isabel and smiles. "Yes, it is a beautiful place," she says. "Stonehenge is from the Neolithic time – it's about 5,000 years old. That's older than the Great Pyramids – the oldest buildings in Egypt. The tallest stones are more than seven metres high. They are called sarsen stones, and they come from here in Wiltshire. The smaller stones are called bluestones – they're from the Preseli Hills in Wales."

A JOURNEY TO THE STONES

At one end – about 70 metres from the circle – stands another huge sarsen stone.

"Why is there only one stone there?" asks Shaheed. "What is that for?"

Miss Novak does not have a book or use her phone. She knows a lot about the stones. "That's the Heel Stone," she says. "On the morning of the summer solstice, the sun comes up over it. The builders of Stonehenge were very intelligent, and they wanted the stones to **align** with the sun at sunrise."

"What's the solstice, Miss Novak?" asks Simon.

"The summer solstice happens on the longest day of the year, and the shortest night," answers Miss Novak. "In the UK, that's usually the 21st of June. Neolithic people built Stonehenge for the winter solstice too. That's the shortest day and longest night, and it's usually on the 21st of December."

"How do you know so much about the stones, Miss?" asks Isabel.

Miss Novak laughs. "Because I love history," she says. "Maybe you'll learn to love it too, Isabel."

CHAPTER THREE
The path around the stones

The students get off the bus, and Miss Novak points to the east. "Do you see that long **area** and those ditches in the ground?" she asks. "That's the Stonehenge Cursus. It's about two miles long. The Neolithic people built it 400 years before Stonehenge. The Cursus aligns with the sunrise at the spring and autumn equinoxes. The equinoxes happen between the solstices – in March and September. The days are as long as the nights at equinox."

"What's the Cursus for, Miss?" asks Shaheed.

"Archaeologists don't know," answers Miss Novak. "But maybe for **ceremonies**."

"What's an archaeologist, Miss Novak?" asks Isabel.

"An archaeologist studies archaeology – that's the study of ancient places," answers Miss Novak.

"That's a nice job!" says Isabel, and Miss Novak smiles.

"The Neolithic people made two large holes – one at the Cursus's east end and one at its west end," she goes on. "The holes align with the solstice sunrise at Stonehenge. There are many barrows around the Cursus. This area of Wiltshire was very important hundreds of years before Stonehenge. The Cursus shows us this."

The students walk to Stonehenge with Miss Novak. The stones stand in a big field, and there is a path around them. Other schoolchildren and tourists walk on the path in front and behind Miss Novak's group. Everyone is talking excitedly and taking photos.

"There are too many people on this path!" says Simon.

"I'm sorry, but you must stay on it," says Miss Novak. "But you can see the stones well from here."

"But I want to walk between them," says Isabel.

"Me too," says Jasmine.

"Then you must come here at the solstice," says Miss Novak, with a smile. "You can walk on the grass then. The solstice is the best time to see Stonehenge."

The students and Miss Novak walk slowly around the visitors' path.

"Those outside stones are really tall, Miss Novak," says Simon.

"You're right, Simon," says Miss Novak. "They're very tall. And they're also very heavy."

"How did the Neolithic people build Stonehenge?" Jasmine asks. Simon, Shaheed, Isabel and the other students are all listening to Miss Novak now.

"Well, there were three **stages** of building," says Miss Novak. "The first stage was digging the ditch. Can you see it? It goes in a circle around the stones and it's 110 metres across. The Neolithic people made it about 5,000 years ago. Archaeologists found cow bones in the bottom of the ditch and some stone **tools**."

Miss Novak smiles. "Then, the Neolithic people brought the bluestones here. They're the smaller stones inside the circle, and they came 150 miles from Wales! The builders made a circle of holes inside the ditch. Today, these are called the Aubrey Holes. Why did they dig them? Archaeologists are not sure – maybe Neolithic people put the bluestones in the holes first and moved them later. Archaeologists found the bones of many people in the Aubrey Holes!"

"Wow!" says Simon. "Why did they bury people there?"

"No one knows," answers Miss Novak.

"How did they bring the bluestones here?" asks Shaheed.

"Maybe the Neolithic people brought them by boat on the sea and then up the River Avon," answers Miss Novak. "Or maybe they pushed and pulled them here."

"What was the second stage, Miss?" asks Simon.

"The second stage of building Stonehenge was the sarsen stones," says Miss Novak. "The Neolithic people brought them from a place called West

THE PATH AROUND THE STONES

Woods, about 4,400 years ago. West Woods is nineteen miles from here. Nineteen miles!" says Miss Novak. "The bluestones are big, but the sarsen stones are huge! One stone needed 200 people to pull it!"

"The Neolithic people made a second 'horseshoe' – a half circle – of sarsen stones inside the first sarsen circle. Then, they lay other sarsens on the standing ones. At the beginning, there were thirty stones on the outside circle."

"It was a beautiful **temple** before," says Jasmine.

"That's right," says Miss Novak. "It was *very* beautiful." She looks back at the stones. "In the third stage of building, from 4,280 to 3,930 years ago, the Neolithic people moved the bluestones inside the sarsens."

"Where did the builders of Stonehenge live?" asks Isabel.

Miss Novak points to the east. "In this important second stage, many people lived at Durrington

THE PATH AROUND THE STONES

Walls. That's two miles from here, next to the River Avon. They built another temple at Durrington Walls with wood, and dug a ditch around it. This is called Woodhenge, and it aligned with the solstice too. Archaeologists found thousands of animal bones in the ground at Durrington Walls because the Neolithic people did a lot of eating and drinking. They had lots of ceremonies. 'Durrington Walls was a place for the living,' said one archaeologist. 'And Stonehenge was a place for the dead.'"

"Then, the Neolithic people started to build the Avenue. And a thousand years later, the Bronze Age people finished it," Miss Novak said. "The Avenue is a big path. It goes from the River Avon to Stonehenge, and that end is aligned with the solstice sunrise. In ancient times, people walked up the Avenue to Stonehenge for the solstice. Because Stonehenge is very high, people could see it from many miles away."

"I want to be one of those people. I want to walk up the Avenue to the huge temple of Stonehenge at the solstice," says Isabel. "How wonderful!"

THE PATH AROUND THE STONES

"WOW, Miss Novak, you really know a lot," says Jasmine.

Miss Novak smiles. "I love Stonehenge," she says. "And I hope you do too. It's a very special place."

The students are nearly at the end of the visitors' path now. They stand behind the Heel Stone.

"Miss, why did you become a history teacher and not an archaeologist?" asks Isabel.

Miss Novak laughs. "I studied history at university because I was good at it at school," she says. "I didn't think about archaeology then. But maybe I'll go back to university and study it later. Everything is possible."

Everything is possible.

"I like Miss Novak," thinks Isabel.

CHAPTER FOUR
The exhibition

"Well, the bus is waiting for us," says Miss Novak. "Let's go back now. We can have lunch, and then you can look at the **exhibition**."

It is hot inside the bus, and there are lots of people. The students and Miss Novak are happy to arrive back at the visitor centre.

"It's warm and sunny outside," Miss Novak says. "Let's sit on these seats here and eat our lunch."

The group sit down. Everyone has sandwiches with them. They all eat their lunch and drink bottles of water or fruit juice.

"Miss, what are those strange little houses?" asks Shaheed, with a sandwich in his hand. He is pointing at some small buildings next to the seats.

"Those are huts," says Miss Novak. "They are part of the exhibition. Neolithic people lived in ancient

huts in Durrington Walls. These huts are new, of course, but they're the same as the ancient huts."

"Can we go inside the huts?" asks Simon.

"Yes," says Miss Novak. "Finish your lunch, then go and look. After that, we'll go to the exhibition hall."

The students quickly eat their lunches and start to visit the huts. Simon and Isabel go inside one.

"The Neolithic people had beds, chairs and a fire in one small room," says Simon.

"I like it," answers Isabel. "I want to live in this hut!"

"Me too!" says Simon. "But only with my dog – no parents!"

They laugh. Then Simon suddenly says, "I'm really sorry, Isabel."

"Why are you sorry?" asks Isabel.

"Because I wasn't nice to you," he answers. "You came to Wiltshire from Birmingham. You had no friends, and you weren't happy. But you were different, and I called you 'city girl'. I was stupid because you're really nice. Can we be friends?"

Isabel smiles. "I'm sorry too. Coming here was a big change for me. I didn't want to come because I loved Birmingham. I missed my old friends, and I didn't want new ones. But today is different. Yes, let's be friends."

Suddenly, Shaheed and Jasmine come into the hut. "We're going to the exhibition hall!" Jasmine says.

Simon and Isabel leave the hut and go with Jasmine. They walk into a huge hall. Miss Novak and the other students are standing in the middle. The walls make a big circle, and a film is playing all around them.

"We're standing in the middle of the stone circle," says Simon. "This is 5,000 years ago!"

The class see men and women with tools in the

THE EXHIBITION

film. There are fires on the ground. There are no sarsens, but there are bluestones.

"Those are Neolithic people. They're building Stonehenge," says Jasmine.

"It looks very cold," says Shaheed. "It's winter."

The students watch the different stages of Stonehenge. They see the area at the time of the ditch and bluestones. Then the film shows the huge sarsen stones. It moves to summer and finishes with the sunrise at a summer solstice ceremony. Hundreds of Neolithic people are watching and shouting. Then the film starts again.

"Wow!" says Isabel. "That's beautiful." She watches the solstice sunrise again and again.

"Let's go on, everyone!" says Miss Novak. "There's lots more to see."

Isabel walks through the exhibition hall with Miss Novak and the other students. She looks at ancient bowls, tools and animal bones. She sees a huge sarsen stone and drawings of Neolithic families in their huts. She learns more about the stones, the Cursus and the Avenue, and the area around them.

She also learns about two famous archaeologists. The first is John Aubrey. In 1666, he made the first plan of Stonehenge and found the holes near the ditch.

"And, of course – now they're called the Aubrey Holes!" Isabel thinks. Then she learns about John Stukeley. About 50 years after Aubrey, Stukeley found the Avenue and the Stonehenge Cursus.

Jasmine is standing next to Isabel and reading the same words.

"It's time to go home, class," says Miss Novak, suddenly. She has her phone in her hand. "The school bus is waiting for us."

The students leave the exhibition hall, and Isabel feels sad.

"I want to come back here," she says, and she looks

back one more time at the visitor centre. "I want to see the stones at solstice."

"Me too," says Jasmine. "Maybe one day, we will."

CHAPTER FIVE
Back home

It is evening now. The bus brings the students home, and Isabel's dad is waiting outside St Anne's School in his car. Isabel opens the door and sits down next to him.

"How was Stonehenge?" Mr Ryan asks. "You look excited."

"Oh, I am, Dad. The stones were great!" Isabel says. "What a wonderful place!"

Isabel **chats** about the stones through the journey home. She chats about them at dinner. After dinner, she usually goes upstairs and chats to her Birmingham friends on her phone. But tonight, she stays with her parents in the living room. She chats more about Stonehenge and does not watch any TV.

Mrs Ryan looks at her husband. "Well, there are many other ancient places in and near Wiltshire," says Mr Ryan. "There's the Avebury stone circle – that's also very famous. And there's Silbury Hill too. It's the biggest man-made hill in Europe. But why did the Neolithic people build it? No one knows!"

"And there are the white horses. People cut them into the hills," says Mrs Ryan. "They're very strange and beautiful."

"I want to see all the ancient places," says Isabel. "But most of all, I want to go back to Stonehenge and see the solstice."

Mr and Mrs Ryan smile. "It's nice to see you happy, Isabel," Mr Ryan says. "We were worried about you after Birmingham."

Isabel goes quiet. She looks at the ground.

"What is it?" says her mum. "What's worrying you? Talk to us."

"You and Dad came here because of me," says Isabel, and suddenly she begins to cry. "You changed all our lives because my grades were bad. But my grades at St Anne's are bad too. I'm a bad student. I get bored in class, and I don't listen. And no one at St Anne's likes me – or they didn't before today."

Mr Ryan puts his arm around Isabel. "Isabel, do you really think that? You're wrong."

"We came here because of my new job," says

Mrs Ryan. "It wasn't because of your grades. We felt bad because you had to leave your friends and your life in Birmingham. It's difficult for you. We know that, and we're very sorry."

"Really?" says Isabel. "You didn't come to Wiltshire because of me?"

Mrs Ryan holds her daughter's hand. "No," she says. "We didn't want to take you from your old school. But we really had to come here. The new job was too good, and we wanted to live in the countryside."

"But you had a good day today," says Mr Ryan. "Did you make some new friends?"

Isabel smiles. "Yes," she says. "People were friendly to me today. Simon said sorry, and Jasmine the nerd was really nice to me."

"Why is Jasmine a nerd?" asks Mr Ryan.

"Because she works really hard in class."

"What's wrong with that?" says Mrs Ryan, and laughs.

Isabel smiles. "Nothing. Jasmine's OK. She wants to see the solstice too."

Two weeks later, it is Isabel's birthday. Mr and Mrs Ryan give her a birthday card.

"Look inside it," says Mrs Ryan.

Isabel opens the card. There is money inside and some writing.

*Your other birthday **present** is a visit to the summer solstice at Stonehenge on Saturday 21st June. You can bring two friends with you.*

Isabel puts her arms around her mum and dad. "Oh, thank you! That's the best present in the world!" she says.

That afternoon, Isabel is sitting next to Jasmine in Miss Novak's history class. They are waiting for Miss Novak to arrive and start the lesson.

"My birthday present is a visit to the solstice at Stonehenge!" Isabel says quietly to Jasmine. "Mum and Dad will take me, and I can bring two friends. Would you like to come?"

"Would I like to come?!" Jasmine laughs. "Yes, of course! Oh, thank you! Thank you! I must ask Mum and Dad, of course, but they'll say yes!"

Isabel turns to Simon and Shaheed.

"You enjoyed our visit to Stonehenge. Do one of you want to come to the summer solstice with us?" she asks. "Mum and Dad are taking me and Jasmine, and we have a seat in the car for one more."

"I can't," says Shaheed, sadly. "My family are going to London that weekend. It's my cousin's 18th birthday."

"I'd like to come," says Simon. "Thank you." He smiles happily at Isabel, and Isabel smiles back.

CHAPTER SIX
The solstice

It is the evening of the solstice. Isabel's mother and father are driving to the visitor centre.

"Look at all these cars!" says Mr Ryan. "They're everywhere. There are hundreds of them on the roads and in the fields."

Dad is right. There are *hundreds* of cars, and there are hundreds – maybe thousands – of people too. There are families with children and dogs. There are men with long hair and women in beautiful long dresses. Everyone is wearing lots of colours. There are also many tourists with their cameras.

"Look at all the people here for the solstice," says her mother. "It's going to be a great night."

"I'm really excited," says Jasmine. She is sitting in the back of the car between Simon and Isabel.

"Me too," says Simon.

Dad drives on to a field and finds a place for the car. They all get out.

"What time is the sunrise?" asks Jasmine.

"The solstice sunrise happens tomorrow morning at 4.44 a.m.," says Mr Ryan.

"So are we going to stay at Stonehenge until the sunrise?" says Isabel. She looks down at her thin summer dress.

"That's right. But I have lots of hot soup to drink," says Mum. She takes a big bag from the car and puts it on her back.

Dad takes another bag and puts it over his arm. "I've got more clothes here. But it's going to be a warm summer night," he says. "And it will be **exciting** with all these people."

There are no buses waiting for them this evening. The family begins walking. There are hundreds of other families around them and many people on the fields too. Everyone walks together. It is a beautiful, warm summer's evening, and the sun is orange and close to the horizon. Isabel can hear music and laughing all around her.

Suddenly, the group come through the trees and see the tall grey stones of Stonehenge on the horizon.

"This is very exciting," says Jasmine to Isabel. "Thank you for bringing me."

Isabel smiles at Jasmine. "You loved it here too," she answers. "I had to bring you."

The group walk across the field until they come to the stones. It is great to walk between the huge sarsens.

"They're so tall!" says Simon. "They looked tall from the path, but now I can really feel it. They're huge!"

It's getting dark now, but the night is warm and lots of people have small lights and their phones. Everyone waits in the dark. Isabel can hear children

THE SOLSTICE

laughing and playing. A young man sits on the grass near her. He's playing a guitar. A woman sits next to him and sings beautifully. Isabel and her friends begin dancing to the music. Then, her mum and dad start dancing too!

The hours pass. The family and Isabel's friends drink the hot soup and eat sandwiches. They put on warmer clothes and dance or walk around. They talk to the other people. "We come to Stonehenge every year for the solstice ceremony," many of the people tell them. "It's a very special time."

Slowly, the sky starts to turn grey. Morning and the sunrise are coming. Everyone is really excited now. "Isabel, Simon and Jasmine!" shouts Isabel's mother. "Let's stand here, opposite the Heel Stone. This is a great place to watch the sunrise!"

The group stand together about 75 metres from the Heel stone. The people are quiet now, and the sky is getting brighter and brighter. Then, suddenly, there is a thin yellow light on the horizon.

"Here comes the sunrise!" someone shouts.

THE SOLSTICE

They all watch the sun move slowly up behind the Heel Stone, until it is "sitting" on top of it. The sky is a bright red, and the clouds are pink and grey. There is shouting, dancing and laughing, and shouts of "happy solstice!" Suddenly, Isabel remembers the film in the exhibition hall. She thinks about Stonehenge 5,000 years ago. There were thousands of people here then too. Maybe there was singing. Maybe there were people from other countries.

"Some things don't change," Isabel says to Simon. "And I'm very happy about that."

THE SOLSTICE

CHAPTER SEVEN
Everything is possible

It is one year later, and Isabel is in her history class. She is sitting with her best friends, Jasmine, Shaheed and Simon, and she holds up a paper. "Look, I got an A!" she shouts. "Thank you, Miss Novak!"

"Don't thank me," says Miss Novak. "You studied very hard this year, Isabel, and your work is very good."

"Because you're a good teacher, Miss Novak," says Isabel.

"Thank you," answers Miss Novak.

"Will you study history at university, Isabel?" asks Simon.

"No," says Isabel.

"Why not?" asks Jasmine. "You love history."

"But I love archaeology more," answers Isabel. "And I want to be an archaeologist."

"That will be difficult," says Shaheed. "It will be four years of studying."

"I know," says Isabel. She smiles at Miss Novak. "But everything is possible."

During-reading questions

CHAPTER ONE

1. Where are the children, and what are they going to visit?
2. Why is Isabel unhappy?

CHAPTER TWO

1. What are the strange hills, and what are they for?
2. How old is Stonehenge, and how tall are the tallest stones?
3. Why is the Heel Stone important at the summer solstice?

CHAPTER THREE

1. What do archaeologists do?
2. Where did the builders of Stonehenge live in the second stage?

CHAPTER FOUR

1. What is inside the hut?
2. Which two famous archaeologists does Isabel learn about?

CHAPTER FIVE

1. What are the other famous ancient places in and near Wiltshire?
2. Why are Isabel's parents sorry?
3. What is Isabel's birthday present? Why is the date important?

CHAPTER SIX

1. Who is in the car with Isabel?
2. "Some things don't change," Isabel says to Simon. Why does she say this, and how does she feel about it?

CHAPTER SEVEN

1. What grade does Isabel get for history?
2. What does Isabel want to study at university?

After-reading questions

1 What were the three stages of building Stonehenge?
2 Who was your favourite person in the story? Why?
3 How does Isabel change in the story?

Exercises

CHAPTER ONE

1 Complete these sentences in your notebook, using the words from the box.

misses	university	stones	worried
	nerd	ancient	

1 She came to Wiltshire from Birmingham with her parents in February, and she ..*misses*.. the city.
2 "I don't want to be in a field of stupid ...."
3 "This is Wiltshire. The countryside here is beautiful and ...."
4 "Mum and Dad were .... about me, and they came to Wiltshire."
5 "She finished .... last year. She's a very new teacher."
6 "Jasmine is a .... ," Isabel thinks.

CHAPTER TWO

2 Write the past tense of these irregular verbs in your notebook.
1. begin *began*
2. bury
3. build
4. see
5. lie
6. stand

CHAPTER THREE

3 Are these sentences *true* or *false*? Write the correct answers in your notebook
1. The Stonehenge Cursus is three miles long. *false The Stonehenge Cursus is about two miles long.*
2. An archaeologist studies English.
3. You can walk on the grass at the solstice.
4. There were two stages of building.
5. The Neolithic people brought the bluestones.
6. The bluestones came from a place called West Woods.

CHAPTER FOUR

4 What happens here? Match in your notebook.
Example: 1 – c

1 On the bus
2 Outside the huts
3 Inside the huts
4 In the exhibition hall

a they eat their lunch.
b the children watch a film.
c it is hot and there are lots of people.
d Simon says sorry to Isabel.

CHAPTER FIVE

5 Complete the sentences in your notebook with the correct form of the verb.

1 The bus ...*brings*..... (**bring**) the students home, and Isabel's dad is ………. (**wait**) outside St Anne's School in his car.
2 Isabel ……….. (**chat**) about the stones through the journey home.
3 "It's nice to see you happy, Isabel," Mr Ryan says. "We were ………. (**worry**) about you after Birmingham."
4 "And no one at St Anne's ………. (**like**) me – or they ………. (**do not**) before today."
5 That afternoon, Isabel is ………. (**sit**) next to Jasmine in Miss Novak's history class.
6 "Do one of you want to ………. (**come**) to the summer solstice with us?"

CHAPTER SIX

6 Write questions for these answers in your notebook.

1 *How many cars are there?*

There are hundreds of cars.

2 ....?

They feel excited.

3 ....?

It happens at 4.44 a.m.

4 ....?

She can hear music and laughing all around her.

5 ....?

It moves slowly up behind the Heel Stone.

6 ....?

She thinks about Stonehenge 5,000 years ago.

CHAPTER SEVEN

7 Look at the picture on page 55, and answer the questions in your notebook.

1 Who can you see in the picture?
2 Where are they?
3 How are they feeling? Why?

Project work

1 You are Isabel. Write a diary page of
   a your school visit to Stonehenge, or
   b the night of the solstice.

2 Look online and learn more about Stonehenge or an ancient building in your own country. Make a poster about it.

3 Write a newspaper report about the night of the solstice.

4 Write a chapter about Isabel's life five years after this story ends.

5 Do people in your country celebrate the solstice? What do they do? Make a presentation about it.

An answer key for all questions and exercises can be found at **www.penguinreaders.co.uk**

Glossary

align (v.)
to put something near another thing. Often, they are in a line.

ancient (adj.)
very old

area (n.)
a part of a place

around (prep.)
in many parts of a place

boring; bored (adj.)
You are *bored* because you are doing nothing, or because you are doing something but you do not like it. It is *boring*.

bury (v.)
to put something under the ground

ceremony (n.)
People come together for something important. Maybe they sing and dance. This is a *ceremony*.

chat (v. and n.)
1) to talk to someone in a friendly way
2) to write messages to another person on the internet. These messages are called *chat*.

countryside (n.)
The *countryside* is not in the town or city. There are many trees and fields in the *countryside*.

exciting; excited (adj.)
You are very happy because you are waiting for an *exciting* thing to happen. You are *excited*.

exhibition (n.)
a big room with pictures and/or interesting things. Lots of people come and see them.

grade (n.)
a number or letter for your work at school. "A" means "very good", "B" means "good", etc.

history (n.)
Things happened before now. This is *history*.

horizon (n.)
The sky meets the Earth at the *horizon*.

huge (adj.)
very big

journey (n.)
You travel from one place to a different place on a *journey*.

miss (v.)
You are sad because you are not in a place. You *miss* the place.

nerd (n.)
A *nerd* enjoys knowing a lot about something. *Nerd* is not always a kind word.

present (n.)
We give people *presents* at Christmas or for their birthday.

really (adv.)
very

seat (n.)
You sit on a *seat*.

stage (n.)
The first *stage* is the first thing you do. The second *stage* is the second thing you do, etc.

stone (n.)
Stone is on or in the ground. It is cold and hard.

suddenly (adv.)
quickly

temple (n.)
A special place. People meet in a *temple* and have *ceremonies* there.

tool (n.)
You hold a *tool* in your hand and use it to build or do other things.

university (n.)
People leave school and go to *university*.

worried (adj.); **worry** (v.)
You are *worried* because maybe something bad will happen. You are *worrying* about something.

Penguin Readers

Visit **www.penguinreaders.co.uk**
for FREE Penguin Readers resources
and digital and audio versions of this book.